The
Promise Doctrine

*A guidebook and system for consistently
delivering on your promises!*

Craig P. Womack
Senior Executive Leader, Speaker, Trainer and Coach

Jason W. Womack, MEd, MA
Professional Workplace Performance Trainer, Coach, and Consultant

Conceived, written and designed in the United States of America. Printed in China.

For information contact jason@womackcompany.com

Book design by Terry Lockman

ISBN:978-0-9842590-0-7

FIRST EDITION

FOREWORD
by Marshall Goldsmith

Ethical behavior is a key characteristic of successful leaders. If people are going to willingly follow a leader, they need to trust that their leaders are going to bring them to a place where they want to be. Today, many people believe that ethics are lacking in their leaders and go so far as to say that ethical behavior will become the most important quality of leaders of the future.

Behind the broad concept of "ethical behavior" is a simple act that a leader can take to build trust: make realistic promises and keep them. You see, leaders are defined by the promises they make and the promises they keep— and the discrepancy between the two. Leaders who make lots of little (or big) promises they don't keep or who negotiate and who tend to renegotiate without fulfilling their promises will soon find that their people are not following, not listening, not trusting, and chances are, not staying.

That's why this book, *The Promise Doctrine*, is so important right now. It puts in your hands a system that will guide you to deliver on your promises. And it's not just about keeping promises on the line or in the board room; it's about being true to your word at home and in your personal life. Because as Jason and Craig say in numerous ways in this great book, doing what you say you're going to do, when you say you're going to do it "encourages achievement, honesty, and teamwork in all areas of life and work." And, who wouldn't want that?

The Promise Doctrine is an extraordinary resource! This guide and activity book is invaluable to anyone leading and living in the 21st century world. Hats off to the authors for producing such a terrific, thoughtful handbook to personal and professional success!

Marshall Goldsmith — million selling author of
"What Got You Here Won't Get You There"
"Succession: Are You Ready?"
and the upcoming "MOJO"

TABLE OF CONTENTS

PREFACE

When we took on this project, a writing collaboration between father and son, we knew that we wanted to explore the dynamics of promise keeping. Over the years of developing our relationship with each other, we noticed that the more we kept our word, both personally and professionally, the stronger our bond grew with each other and with others.

As we continued to study the effects of how commitments (whether kept, broken, or renegotiated) impacted virtually every human interaction and relationship, we began to understand the power of a promise.

The Promise Doctrine was developed from our vision of providing a simple but powerful guidance system for the processes that go into keeping your word. By keeping track of your promises and having control over what you've said "yes" to, you can put yourself in a great position to quantify what you're doing and to actually see your accomplishments.

The Promise Doctrine is organized around focusing on the importance of promises and the Six Elements of promise keeping. We've included QuickTips and QuickTip Details with suggestions to help you apply and use the Six Elements.

When doing research for our book, we were overwhelmed by the numerous responses we received to the following question: "When I make a promise, what I mean is..."

While we have included a number of these quotes in the back of this book, one sums up why it is time for *The Promise Doctrine.*

Art Carden, Assistant Professor of Economics and Business, Rhodes College, wrote:

"When I make a promise, what I mean is..."

1. Ideally, most of us would answer: "...that I will deliver on what was asked for in the time in which it is wanted." This is what I want to mean.

2. Realistically, I think most of us would answer: "...that I will think about how nice it would be to deliver what has been asked for in the time it is wanted, but what I will do is realize as the deadline approaches that there is no way I'm going to finish what I planned to do by the deadline. So I'll probably ask for an extension, all the while apologizing profusely for my inability or unwillingness to recognize my limitations."

We wrote this book for people who want to make Art's **ideal** their reality.

ACKNOWLEDGEMENTS

There are several people who helped us get this book into your hands. We turned to them for ideas, support, feedback and editorial advice.

From Craig

My wife, Gail, has always encouraged me to write. Her support and counsel throughout *The Promise Doctrine* project was the inspirational, motivational, and reassuring spark that kept me moving forward. Content is a culmination of life's experiences, decisions, interactions, emotions, relationships, triumphs, setbacks, conversations, and more.

Thank you to all of the folks that I have had the privilege of sharing life moments, working with, and knowing. Special thanks to Michael and Carlene Hamm, Fred Long, Dave and Linda Rossi, Marilyn Snider, Spar Street, Jon Pheils, Brad White, and Wayne and Colleen Womack.

I am truly fortunate to have been able to work with a gifted writing partner who is also my son. Jason, this has been a remarkable ride.

From Jason:

First, a thank you to my friend and life partner, Jodi Womack. You showed me how to get started, and continue focusing on what I can do to be at my best in each moment.

Thank you to my triathlon mentor and friend, Quanah Ridenour. Every day you demonstrate what it is like to live a purposeful life. I now believe that more than I ever thought *is possible*.

Thank you to my colleague, fellow teacher, and family man, Joe Bruzzese. Publishing your book, and helping people worldwide inspires me to want to do more and more each day.

And, finally, thanks Dad! I think this book really DID take almost 4 decades to write; and, I know it was worth it!

CHAPTER
1
What's On Your Promise "Plate"?

Tony did *not* know which way to turn.

Last night he had made a plan. The clock radio was set for 6:30 AM. He wanted to shower and shave, put on a nice suit for work, and eat a somewhat healthy breakfast. He even thought he would have time to catch up on the news feeds from Google and the New York Times.

However, the plan was *not* working. After pressing "snooze" twice, he was jolted awake by Phil Collins singing *"No Way Out."*

Hurriedly, he took a shower, cut himself while shaving, found a wrinkled suit in the back of the closet, and microwaved yesterday's coffee for breakfast.

A familiar voice asked, "what else could possibly go wrong?" He looked at the laptop bag in his hand, knew he wasn't prepared and drove to work.

Stopped at a red light, Tony thought, "How did this happen?" This was the day of the big presentation, and he was not ready.

How do promises begin?

Three weeks ago, Tony promised to present a comprehensive review of his company's competition to the Executive Committee.

In that meeting, he had eagerly raised his hand signaling that he would take on this assignment. "This" he thought, "is something that could get the attention of the CEO and other key executives in the company, and make me look good."

Tony knew that he had to do something extraordinary to be considered for a promotion. This was his big opportunity and he wasn't going to let it pass him by.

He now realized that his desire for recognition and advancement had overshadowed the reality of the scope and complexity of the project. He hadn't taken into consideration all of the other things that he had said "yes" to, both in his personal life and at work. He now found himself to be overwhelmed with the current work project and had reached a point of paralysis. He had made a promise to present the findings today, and he was in trouble.

Promises begin the moment you say
"yes" to yourself or to others

Promises impact others

As scheduled at 10 AM, Tony entered the conference room. The executives of the company, including the CEO, were already in the room and awaiting his presentation.

All eyes turned towards Tony. Buckets of sweat formed on his forehead as he thought about all of the time he had wasted and spent on low priority tasks over the past three weeks. He began reaching and searching for some inspirational epiphany. *None came.*

"I can't believe it," Tony thought, "I'm going to let them down, too." Looking at no one in particular, he announced he wasn't prepared and that he had completely underestimated the complexity and size of the project.

The CEO turned a judgmental yet constructive eye towards Tony and asked just three questions:

"Why did you wait until today to tell us that you couldn't deliver as promised?"

"How much more time would you need to complete the project?"

"If we move forward, who will you go to for help?"

Tony hoarsely responded, "I missed today's deadline because I got so overwhelmed with the idea of making a perfect presentation that I became paralyzed by the scope of the project. I thought I could talk my way through it. I thought I could do the project on my own and that, obviously, was a mistake. If given a second chance, I will need three more weeks to identify my resources, interview the appropriate people, do the research and have the presentation finalized."

There was an insufferable moment of silence before the CEO responded, "I'm disappointed that you didn't ask for help and are unable to present the report to us today, as we had expected. We certainly could have used our time more effectively this morning. I will expect you to be ready to present a comprehensive and completed project in three weeks, if you're up for it."

Unkept promises waste everyone's time, energy, and focus

Know your lifelines AND use them!

Tony had just been handed a "time" lifeline from the CEO. Tony also understood that he needed to get help to complete the project.

He knew that for the next three weeks, he would use every "resource" lifeline available to him. He would dedicate the time needed to get his study of the competition completed. For the first time, Tony felt the judgment of "asking for help" slip away. He began to realize the executive skill of managing information and resources.

*Did you know it's okay to
ask for help?*

Break it down into actionable steps

When he got back to his office, Tony toweled down, sat upright in his office chair and wrote out his plan of action for the next three weeks. This included putting together web and product research on competitors, setting up Google Alerts, meeting with four co-workers knowledgeable about the company's competitors, a visit to the local book store for more research, and asking for help from his contacts on LinkedIn and Facebook.

*You have access to more
information than you think,
if you'll think that way*

Three weeks later

Tony looked in the mirror to see a determined and confident face...his!

The day was already very different from that one three weeks ago. He woke up at 6:30 AM to *"It's a Beautiful Morning,"* by the Rascals. The shower felt great and the shave was clean. He put on the neatly pressed slacks and shirt which were laid out and ready. Breakfast consisted of a bowl of oatmeal, glass of orange juice and a freshly brewed cup of Peet's coffee. He reviewed his presentation one more time, put his computer in the laptop bag and drove to work.

This was the day of the big presentation, and he was not only ready, he was pumped. He had made a promise to himself and the executive team; today, he was determined to deliver on that promise.

At 9:45 AM, he gathered up his materials, which included a meticulously prepared PowerPoint presentation and 10 handout copies (printed on two sides) and walked towards the conference room with a new level of determined confidence.

Promptly at 10 AM, he made eye contact with his CEO and said with controlled enthusiasm, "Now, let's talk about our competition."

Magic happens when
you keep your promises

CHAPTER

2

Why This, Why Now?

Relationships, families,
businesses and organizations are
defined by the promises people keep,
break, and renegotiate

The *Promise Doctrine* is a guidebook and system for consistently delivering on your promises.

We considered writing another book with motivational philosophies, go-for-the-gusto goal setting programs, inspirational slogans and a biography or two of successful leaders who have "made it."

We took a different course.

With this book in your hands, you hold a system that puts you clearly and fundamentally in control of your promises. Read and apply the elements of *The Promise Doctrine* to achieve more than you thought possible.

Again and again, people are searching for the secret to success, personally and professionally. Our work is based on one central principle:

Do what you say you're going to do, when you say you're going to do it

Seemingly simple, this philosophy encourages achievement, honesty, and teamwork in all areas of life and work.

Yes, *The Promise Doctrine* applies to your personal life and your work life. Audiences small and large, around the world, have applied the elements of *The Promise Doctrine*. We work with health care providers, schools and universities, banks, retail companies, non profit organizations, and many other groups and foundations.

We live in a remarkable era with the opportunity to improve, re-set and amplify our values of responsibility and accountability. Identifying what is important to you and acting on that will take your time, energy and focus.

We believe that personal responsibility is the foundation of achievement

In our seminars, we ask people to share what comes to mind when they see the letters PR. They usually share the following:

public relations, pride, provide

Upon further reflection people add:

productivity, program, pronto, process, progress, prove, preview, precedent, pressure, promote, proliferate, procrastinate, proceed, proactive, prudent, procure, produce, prioritize, pronounce, promise

_____ _____ _____

_____ _____ _____

_____ _____ _____

_____ _____ _____

Take the next 30 seconds to circle (and add to the list as other words come to mind) any of the PR words that mean something to you. (*The Promise Doctrine* book is designed as a guide and activity book. On several pages, you will find room to take notes and capture your ideas, so keep that pen or pencil handy.)

These PR words *can* describe actions, activities and outcomes influenced by an individual's value system, concept of fair play, hard work, curiosity, personal responsibility and personal accountability.

Personal responsibility depends upon the fusion of planning and doing

If most of the words that you circled (or wrote) are nouns (public relations, productivity, precedent, etc.) you are likely a "planner," easily visualizing what things will look like, when they are done.

If most of the words that you circled (or wrote) are verbs (provide, process, proceed, etc.) you are likely a "doer," easily and naturally taking action to make things happen.

The two most important words (translated into any language) relating to personal responsibility are:

I Promise

If you have been looking for the "key" to personal and professional success, here it is:

Make important promises, and keep them

CHAPTER

3

So, Let's Get Started

Let's start at the beginning

Please fill in the following lines:

Today's Date:

April 29, 2020

Where I got my copy of *The Promise Doctrine*:

A presentation years ago

Why I'm interested in *The Promise Doctrine*:

I want to feel good about
myself and how I am
showing up both personally
and professionally.
I want to start being
impeccable with my word

As you have already experienced in Chapter 2, we're asking you to write in this book. We know that getting things out of your head and on to paper makes them more real.

For example, when you look at this book a year from now, you'll have a record of when, where, and why you discovered *The Promise Doctrine*.

We encourage you to use *The Promise Doctrine* as an everyday tool to help guide you through the psychology of and system for keeping your promises.

Match your word to your actions

You know the importance of matching your word to your actions, and so do we. We promise to share practical, doable, and repeatable processes that you can use to make and keep important promises.

We value your time and use of resources, and if you've already read this far, we congratulate you and by all means keep on going!

Carry this book with you for at least the next 14 days

Make notes, fold over the corners of specific, important, and memorable pages, and fill in the blank lines of the activities we have provided.

Every page of
"The Promise Doctrine"
provides tools, prompts, and
guides that clear the path
for promise making
and promise keeping

CHAPTER
4

Promise Making

Making promises
to yourself and others,
and then keeping those promises,
reaches across
all life and work boundaries

Exercise #1. The Promise-People Test

Do you still have something to write with? Good. Take just a moment and complete this exercise:

Write down the names of all of the people in your life (work and home) who consistently do what they say they're going to do, when they say they're going to do it. These are the folks that you can always count on to keep their word.

Cheryl — my spouse

Dad

Jim — My former boss and new colleague

Bill

Brent (to some degree)

If people you know were doing this activity, wouldn't it be special if your name was on their list?

The art and science of making promises

Most businesses have a strategy based on company wide goals coupled with actions needed to help the company achieve those goals. This is often referred to as a "Strategic Plan."

While most of us don't have a specifically defined personal "Strategic Plan," we do lead lives based on goals and promises. Every goal, every promise, depends on taking action and achieving milestones.

Promise Keeping is not an accident

In business as well as in your personal life, consitently making and keeping promises depends upon your system and process of managing your word.

If you're like most people who read *The Promise Doctrine*, you're looking to achieve more. We have found that when people objectify, plan and manage their goals, they do achieve more.

When you think of a new goal or making a promise, what are the first things that come to mind? We recommend that you always think about goals and promises in a SMART way.

S - Specific
M - Meaningful
A - Actionable
R - Realistic
T - Timely

Once you've set a SMART promise, determine clear actions and milestones. For each, identify a timetable, person responsible, and the clear objective.

For example:
By (date)_____

(someone)_____
(this can also be team members with a lead)

(will do something)_____

Promises are Powerful

An example of a SMART Promise would be:

Develop the Promise Doctrine Seminar based on *The Promise Doctrine* book.

Examples of milestones for this Promise would be:

By October 1, Jason, Craig and Terry (with Jason as the lead) will build a PowerPoint presentation to support the initial four hour *Promise Doctrine* Seminar/Workshop

By October 15, Craig and Jason (with Craig as the lead) will produce a Workbook to support the initial *Promise Doctrine* Seminar/Workshop

Timeframes

We suggest that you set timeframes for milestones to within a six month window. This will help you deal with the speed of life and to have a realistic path to completion. If longer term milestones are appropriate, certainly include those. We're simply suggesting to stay as close to the target as possible.

Exercise 2. Promises Made:

Write down 2 *significant* promises that you have made in the past month.

Promise 1.

_____

_____

_____

_____

_____

_____

Promise 2.

_____

_____

_____

_____

_____

Here's an example of what a significant promise might look like:

Learn some *conversational* Italian for a trip that is planned for 6 months from now.

Exercise 3. How are these Promises Coming Along?

Write down 2 - 3 updates related to milestones needed to deliver on these promises:
Promise 1. Milestone Updates:

1. _____

_____

2. _____

_____

3. _____

_____

Promise 2. Milestone Updates:

1. _____

_____

2. _____

_____

3. _____

_____

CHAPTER

5

The Promise Journey

You've heard the saying "success is not a destination..." Well, promise keeping is not a singular event. It is something that you continually refine and practice. Promise keeping, much like success, is a journey, not a destination.

When new goals are set and
new promises are made,
we begin a journey to another level

Along the path of developing yourself, both personally and professionally, much of what you read and hear is common sense. *The Promise Doctrine* is the guide you can use to put that common sense into action.

The Promise Journey:
clarify what you've said "yes" to,
clear a path,
achieve measurable results

The Promise Doctrine provides a practical approach to promise making and promise keeping.

Putting ideas into action is a key to success, both in life and at work

In the "real world"

Every day, your priorities change, forcing you to move between, and balance, multiple areas of focus. For example, has a phone call from home or an email from the boss ever changed what you were about to do?

The "Stress" of Opportunity

Successfully managing your changing priorities requires that you begin to organize and systematize the way you approach achieving results.

When you set new goals you take ownership of making positive changes in your life.

Depending on the level of change (a new job or career, a move, a change in family status), you may face hardships, challenges, and new opportunities. Many times, acknowledging that there could be *more* is stressful.

This is more than okay. In fact, like a stressed muscle repairs itself and grows back stronger, the "stress" of opportunity is actually what teaches us and prepares us for the "next time."

It's not that you need to be "out" (out of work, out of love, out of goals, out of gas) to benefit from The Promise Doctrine

You only need to feel or think that things could be different and better

*Improve your productivity and
ability to make and keep more
promises, to yourself and to others,
with the right Tools and Habits*

Tools

The definition of the word "tool" is: a device used to carry out a particular function. So, as you prepare yourself for *The Promise Journey*, identify the gear and tools you depend on and upgrade where necessary.

The best way to find out if you have the right tools is to do an inventory. Try this: for the next three days, write down the name of every tool you use to get things done on the job and in your life. It will help to over-do this list.

Literally, if you commute, write down: car, bus, train, ferry, plane, etc. If you use email, write down: Internet, computer, BlackBerry, iPhone, etc. If you are in a paper-rich environment, write down: printer, fax machine, piles, files, shelves, etc.

Once you have a complete list (and trust us, it will take a few days to get it all), you can begin to evaluate what works and what doesn't work. Keep what works and prepare to change what doesn't work.

Have the right tools!

Habits

A habit is defined as a settled or regular tendency or practice.

The habits you have put into place, sometimes years ago, often drive your actions, focus, and results.

Change your habits, change your life

Once you open your eyes in the morning, your body and mind seek familiarity and routine. Much of what you do is on cruise control, it doesn't need to be on a to-do list, but always gets done.

Examples of habits at work include: how you manage your agreements, tasks and to-dos, how you commute to work, where you go for lunch, what you do when you sit down at your desk and how you motivate yourself to stop, focus and concentrate on a single priority.

Examples of habits at home include: how you manage your agreements, tasks and to-dos, how you start the day, how meals and activities are organized and how you motivate yourself to stop, focus and concentrate on a single priority.

The habit of "The Promise Doctrine": Take personal responsibility, do what you said you were going to do when you said you would do it

Practice the right habits!

*Your personal and professional
success is directly proportional
to your ability to make and
keep your promises*

Gap Management

In our work, we focus on the journey of promise keeping and closing the gap between "knowing" and "doing." Many times, people know what they should be doing, but for some reason (motivation, procrastination, limited resources, etc.) they don't actually get around to it.

In life or in business, people hold images in their minds of what success will look like when they get "there." Occasionally, individual clients and seminar participants share the feeling that they are not making enough progress; that they are not as far along as they think they should be by now. They know they want more but don't know how to get "there." Can *you* relate?

We have heard this from parents looking forward to their children going to college, entrepreneurs anticipating the day they sell their business, couples deciding to get married, managers earning that next promotion, and more.

We all hear and use terms like adaptability, flexibility, challenge, team and productivity. We have an innate desire to please, to help, and to achieve. These desires manifest themselves in wanting to say "yes" and to make promises.

*With the power of the right promises
made and kept, we improve
the journey that our lives take, the
personal relationships that we form,
and the quality of our work.*

We wrote this book to show you how to enjoy the
ride and succeed on your own path of *The Promise
Journey.*

**Are you ready,
Just turn the page...**

CHAPTER

6

The Promise Doctrine

The Six Elements
of The Promise Doctrine

Promise

Promises, with yourself and others, are already in motion.

Every promise that is made requires planning, action, and attention. Some promises need a more structured planning and follow-up process. For those: write them down, identify actions and milestones, and use a "check in" system to achieve the positive results you're after.

Perform

Show up, do great work, repeat.

You are always judged on what you do, not what you say you will do. With each positive performance confidence builds, and it's easier to take on more. Continually train, learn, and develop yourself as a high performer through professional guidance and skills-based coaching. At the end of each day, look back and know you did great work.

Hurdles

Hurdles, the chance to step back, re-set, and move forward.

Life is hard. Along *The Promise Journey,* you will face challenges large and small. Stop complaining and view them as opportunities. Review your plan, identify new actions, and generate positive momentum. Every hurdle you overcome is a new reference bookmark on your navigation bar.

Renegotiate

When things go wrong, reach out to make them right.

Just because you know what to do, and even if you're doing it, positive results are not guaranteed. At times, you may need to renegotiate previously agreed upon terms. Determine what you will need to succeed (more time, more resources, more ideas, etc) and let the right people know as soon as possible.

Trust

Trust your team. Trust your partner. Trust yourself.

The more deposits that you can make into your "trust" bank account - that is, the more you do what you said you would do - trust builds and relationships strengthen. Truth is, people like people who keep their word.

Celebrate

On your way to your next success, pause long enough to reflect on and celebrate this one!

Celebrating achievements, large and small, builds momentum, creates a positive mind set and fuels the inspiration to continue. Making and keeping promises feels real good, and it just feels right!

The impact of doing
what you say you're going to do,
when you say you will do it,
puts a halo around the words:
"I Promise"

When your "yes" means "yes," and you do what you say you're going to, life gets better

Making promises, balancing your needs with the needs of others, and doing what you say you're going to do, creates a rock-solid platform for further achievement, increased confidence, and real-world credibility.

Strengthen your integrity quotient by
keeping your promises,
on time, and every time

Do you know everything you have said "yes" to? Really, *every single thing?* Most people have made to-do lists that represent today's issues, crises or priorities.

Give yourself the gift of your own attention

It's time to do a mindsweep

Let's get a current snapshot of just how much you have actually said "yes" to. Sit down, find something to write with, and listen to the answers that come to your mind when you ask yourself this question:

"What are all the things I have said 'yes' to?"

Write as fast as you can, get as many out of your head as possible. Big or little, personal or professional, long-term, or short-term, get them all!

This may be the most complete inventory of the commitments you have made, to yourself and to others, that you have ever seen in your life.

On the next two pages, we have provided a mindsweep form for you to use now. There is also a list of potential areas of focus to get you started.

Go for it! Fill in as many lines as possible.

(For electronic copies of the mindsweep form, visit: www.ThePromiseDoctrine.com)

6

The Promise Doctrine

Potential areas of focus

Projects to start planning

People to talk to - topic

Meetings to plan/think about

Books/magazines to read

Volunteer/Community

Children/Family/Parents

Trips to plan/take

Rest/Relaxation

Classes to take/lectures to attend

Systems/Programs to learn

Supplies/Tools/Gear to buy

Workspace set up issues to resolve

Anything else?

Simply answer this question:

"What have I said 'yes' to?"

Today's Date

_____

MINDSWEEP

(For electronic copies of the mindsweep form, visit:
www.ThePromiseDoctrine.com)

Okay, just one more form, "The Promise Guide"

(Below is a thumbnail version. Open to the back of your book, fold out the back pages, and you will find a full sized *Promise Guide*)

The Promise Guide			
Promise	Milestones	🏆	Comments or Course Correction

The Promise Guide is a blueprint and tracking guide you can use to document, manage and follow up on the bigger, long term promises you want to make or have made. *The Promise Guide* is not a substitute for the to-do lists that you already have. Don't worry, we'll show you how to use it in just a minute.

(For electronic copies of the *Promise Guide* form, visit: www.ThePromiseGuide.com)